Derbysh...
Wildlife T...

Wildlife
Walks

Protecting **Wildlife** for the Future

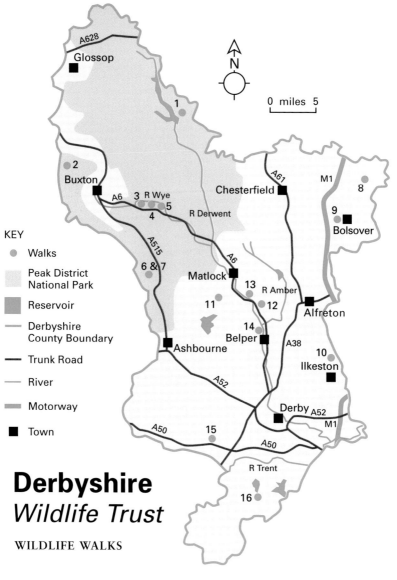

Derbyshire
Wildlife Trust

WILDLIFE WALKS

CONTENTS

Wildlife Walks
Published by Derbyshire Wildlife Trust
2006. © All rights reserved
Derbyshire Wildlife Trust,
East Mill, Bridge Foot, Belper,
Derbyshire, DE56 1XH.
www.derbyshirewildlifetrust.org.uk

We are grateful to Aggregate Industries
and the Appletree Hundred Group of
Derbyshire Wildlife Trust for their
financial support of this book.

Illustrations: Daniel Rodrigues
                 and Jackie Farrand
Photographs: Mark Hamblin
Design: Mike Blaver Design

ISBN: 1-871444-03-9
Printed by: Cromwell Press Ltd,
Trowbridge

Redstart

Using this book

*T*he walks in this book vary in length and difficulty. Some are suitable for all the family, while others should only be attempted by reasonably fit adults. Please refer to the guidance at the start of each route description for more information.

Sketch maps are provided for each walk, but these are intended to act as a quick guide only and you are advised to take the relevant Ordnance Survey map with you, as indicated in the details for each route.

The routes describe the practicalities of getting around the walk, and also include information on the wildlife you can expect to see - this will vary from season to season, and where possible we have indicated the best time of year to undertake each walk and what you can expect to see. You will find a pair of binoculars and a relevant field guide helpful.

Some nature reserves are secluded and well off the beaten track, and not directly accessible by public transport. However we have, where practical, attempted to include details of bus or train routes nearby.

Please make sure that you have appropriate clothing and footwear for the route and that you follow the Countryside Code:

- Be safe - plan ahead and follow any signs.
- Leave gates and property as you find them.
- Protect plants and animals, and take your litter home.
- Keep dogs under close control and on a lead wherever there is livestock or if requested by the landowner.
- Consider other people.

We would like to thank all the volunteers who have devised and checked routes for us and who give up their spare time to help us look after our nature reserves.

*Green
Woodpecker*

Derbyshire Wildlife Trust

*D*erbyshire Wildlife Trust is the leading organisation working to protect wildlife throughout the county. As a registered charity, we rely heavily on the support of our members and volunteers to help us carry out our aim of protecting Derbyshire's wildlife for the future.

The Trust currently manages 40 nature reserves right across the county. They vary from the majestic and internationally important limestone dale woodlands of Chee Dale, Priestcliffe Lees and Miller's Dale - known collectively as the Wye Valley Reserves - to gravel pits teeming with bird life at Hilton in the south of the county.

In addition to nature reserves, the Trust works in many other areas. Our education staff visit schools to encourage children, their teachers and parents to become interested in the natural world. Schools also visit our Whistlestop Countryside Centre, where expert staff help them experience nature at first hand, through nature walks, pond dipping and other activities.

We also work with local authorities, advising them on the likely environmental impact of planning applications. We maintain the Register of County Wildlife Sites, which lists areas in the county outside the Peak District National Park, which are not nature reserves but which contain habitats and species that are locally or nationally important. Our Wildlife Sites Officers visit owners of these sites to advise them on how to manage their land in the best interests of the wildlife.

Certain species and habitats have been identified through Biodiversity Action Plans as in special need of action to guarantee their future. The Trust works with local authorities and other partner organisations to secure the future of some of these. Through species monitoring and action we have begun to see positive signs of the otter's return to Derbyshire and have helped ensure the survival of the native black poplar tree. We continue to raise awareness and take appropriate action to reverse the dramatic decline in water vole numbers in the county, and work to ensure that the last of our precious wildflower meadows do not disappear for ever.

These are just some of the projects the Trust has been involved in.
Many other projects are planned for the future - and many of the species
and habitats we seek to protect can be found on the walks in this book.
We hope that you enjoy them.

Nature Reserves
in Derbyshire

*D*erbyshire Wildlife Trust's nature reserves are located throughout the county. Wherever you live or are staying in Derbyshire, there is likely to be a reserve within easy reach.

Nature reserves are not parks, neither are they zoos where you are almost guaranteed to see creatures in close proximity. They are wild places, which are carefully managed in appropriate and sensitive ways for the benefit, first and foremost, of the habitats and species found there. We also endeavour to make them visitor-friendly, and have created paths and installed boardwalks on several reserves to enable visitors to enjoy the natural beauty safely and without disturbing it.

However, it is necessary to restrict access to some reserves in order to protect particularly vulnerable wildlife, and in some cases because allowing public access would be too dangerous. For some of these reserves, permits are available from our office for a small fee. At others, access to the reserve is not possible, but viewing areas are provided from adjacent paths.

We ask that dog owners keep their animals on a lead to prevent disturbance of wildlife and the livestock which we use to graze our nature reserves. If you see anything during your visit that concerns you, or you would like to arrange for a large party (12 people or more) to visit one of our reserves, please contact us at the Trust office.

Enjoy your walk.

Jacob's Ladder

Habitats in Derbyshire

*D*erbyshire lies at the boundary of upland and lowland Britain and is influenced by both the humid north western and the drier south eastern climates. As a result it has one of the greatest range of habitats and species of any inland county in the British Isles. From the gritstone moorland and blanket bog of the north of the county; through the limestone dales; the coal measures and magnesian limestone of the east; over the flood plains of the Trent Valley; and onto the rolling claylands in the very south, our county has a remarkable variety to offer wildlife enthusiasts. The walks described in this book are chosen to help you enjoy the richness of Derbyshire's wildlife.

GRASSLAND

The grasslands of Derbyshire are as varied as the county. The grasslands of the limestone dalesides are some of the best flower-rich areas in Europe which in turn support a wide array of invertebrates. To experience the variety of life that these areas have to offer, try the Chee Dale, Deep Dale and Priestcliffe Lees walk. Lead mining in the White Peak has left its mark in the form of shafts and lead spoil heaps. The spoil heaps support a special grassland which is tolerant of heavy metals and contains two flowers known as 'leadwort' - spring sandwort and alpine penny cress. Gang Mine Nature Reserve, which features in one of our walks, is an example of this type of grassland.

Priestcliffe Lees SSSI.

Wet grasslands in the flood plains provide nesting habitat for nationally declining birds such as the lapwing and provide grazing and refuge for winter wildfowl like the wigeon - try out our walks around Erewash Meadows and Wyver Lane to see some of these bird species.

Acid grasslands on the moorland fringe, whilst often underrated, support a notable range of fungi as well as flowers like the heath spotted orchid.

Long Clough.

WOODLAND

Derbyshire has a relatively low proportion of woodland. In the south, the National Forest is now restoring areas of woodland. In the uplands, woodland tends to be limited to more inaccessible areas where agricultural improvement and clearance have not been viable.

Some small remaining areas of oak woodland cling on to the steeper sides of the gritstone valleys in the Peak District. Here you are likely to see birds such as the pied flycatcher, which still occur in good numbers, as well as the purple hairstreak butterfly which flits around at canopy level. These are just two of the rich variety of species which occur in ancient oak woods. Look at the mosses, fungi and ferns and the invertebrates in the leaf litter.

Mountain Currant Flower.

Our walk around Hillbridge Wood is the best way to experience our oak woodlands - visit in spring when the woodland floors are carpeted with bluebells.

The ash woodland in the limestone dales comes into leaf very late and has a well-lit woodland floor with a high number of flowers and shrubs. Mountain currant and mezerion, two of the rarer shrubs, can be seen alongside the more common guelder rose, dogwood and purging buckthorn, which is the food plant of the stunning brimstone butterfly. Columbine, globe flower and lily of the valley are three of the more special flowers of the woodland floor.

Ladybower Wood SSSI.

Try our walks in the Wye Valley around Chee Dale and Priestcliffe Lees for the best daleside woodland.

Chee Dale SSSI.

Hillbridge Wood.

WETLAND

Numerous rivers and streams that flow down from the Derbyshire Peaks and through lowland Derbyshire provide a whole range of habitats. In addition, human activity has also created significant wetland features from reservoirs to canals, mineral extraction to mining subsidence.

Carr Vale Flash.

Open water pools, reedbeds and marshes occur mostly in the east and south of the county. Canals, reservoirs, sand and gravel extraction and mining subsidence have provided good areas of wetland which support a significant range of birds, plants, invertebrates and mammals. Our walk around Carr Vale gives you an ideal opportunity to see how mining subsidence has resulted in a wetland area which is now among the best birdwatching sites in the county.

Hilton Gravel Pits SSSI.

MOORLAND

A large proportion of land in North Derbyshire is made up of Pennine moors. The vistas of purple heather in late summer offer the most endearing memories of Derbyshire's moorlands. Spring also has a few pleasures to offer, especially when the golden plover, whinchat and other birds are breeding and when the emperor moth is on the wing. Our walk at Ladybower Wood offers the best opportunities to enjoy moorland scenery and wildlife.

Emperor Moth.

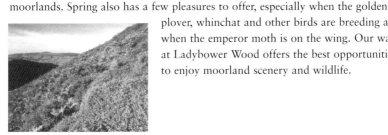

Overdale.

Derbyshire has significant areas of bare rock habitat, because of its geology both in the White and Dark Peak. Post-glacial conditions not only created the impressive limestone gorges but are believed to have created the scree slopes, a significant feature in some dales and in the vast sand and gravel areas in the Trent Valley.

Supporting lichens, ferns, mosses as well as a range of plants and invertebrates of ledges and crevices, bare rock - both vertical and more horizontal - is a very obvious part of the gritstone and limestone areas of Derbyshire. Whether in the form of vertical cliffs, horizontal bed rock, scree slopes, or streamside boulders there is wildlife that depends on that rock. Much of that wildlife is not very obvious, but is an important part of the food webs and the wildlife communities of the habitats. Our walk through Chee Dale provides some excellent examples of vertical limestone cliffs.

Bare rock and earth in lowland Derbyshire, usually the result of mineral extraction, provides nest sites for birds such as the oystercatcher and nesting burrows for animals as diverse as solitary wasps and shelduck.

Chee Dale SSSI.

Volunteering

As a charity, the Trust depends on volunteers to help us in every aspect of our work. Volunteers have checked and written many of the routes in this book, for example.

The task of looking after all our nature reserves - mowing, raking, maintaining paths, pulling rhododendron, clearing scrub etc - would be a mammoth one without the help of our army of volunteers. A regular Mid Week Team visits reserves to carry out maintenance and survey work, while many reserves have volunteer managers who organise weekend work parties once a month.

Volunteering has many benefits - you can learn new skills, get outdoors and become more active. It's a good way to meet people with similar interests and if you are between jobs it is a useful addition to your CV.

No specific skills are necessary to begin volunteering on a nature reserve - all you need is enthusiasm, a reasonable level of fitness and the appropriate clothing.

If you are not able to help on a reserve but would still like to be involved, we need volunteers in all aspects of our work. Volunteers help out in our Whistlestop Countryside Centre shop in Matlock Bath, provide administrative support in our offices and represent us at events. Our seven local groups are run by volunteers who also attend local shows.

If you are interested in volunteering, contact the Trust office to find out more or visit our website.

Water Vole

Ladybower Wood

A walk in the Dark Peak with superb views, taking in oak woodland, heather moorland and gritstone tors with a return along the wooded side of large reservoirs. *By Steve Price.*

Redstart

START/
PARKING:
: Heatherdene car park, 1½ miles north of the village of Bamford on the A6013. Grid ref SK 202858.

DISTANCE:
: 13 miles/21km - by studying the map other paths down from the edge to the valley bottom can be used to create a number of shorter circular routes.

DIFFICULTY:
: Steep in parts, rough underfoot, exposed to all weathers. Please note: whilst on distinct paths, this walk takes you over high open moorland (maximum altitude 538m) and all walkers at all times of year should be adequately equipped for walking in bad weather.

OS MAP:
: 1:25,000 scale Outdoor Leisure 1 - The Peak District - The Dark Peak Area. Note: it is essential that users of this walk consult and carry this map.

TOILETS:
: At the car park.

PUBLIC
TRANSPORT:
: Castleton - Sheffield buses pass the start point. Glossop - Sheffield buses stop at the Ladybower Inn (1km north of the start point), an alternative start.

LOOK FOR:
: Birds including ring ouzel, golden plover, red grouse, pied flycatcher and wood warbler in spring; emperor moth in summer; heather at its finest in late summer; mountain hares in winter.

NOTE:
: If the wind is from the north-east it is suggested that the route be completed in the reverse direction to keep the wind to your back when on the open moor.

1 Leave the car park and turn right along the A6013 to walk alongside the Ladybower Reservoir. After ⅓ mile turn right at the T-junction with the A57. Cross the front of the Ladybower Inn to take the bridle track which branches off uphill to the left.

2 Follow this bridle track ahead as it climbs alongside and then through a gate into the Ladybower Wood Nature Reserve. *Keep your eyes open in summer for the purple hairstreak butterfly which uses the oak canopy to breed. At this point look across the valley at the very steep woodland of Derbyshire Wildlife Trust's Priddock Wood Nature reserve. This oak woodland is north facing and supports a different range of plants to the south facing and drier Ladybower Wood.*
At a fork in the track keep to the main right branch. Ahead, just beyond a very shallow ford, pass through a gate across the track to leave the nature reserve.

3 Continue ahead on the bridle track across more open country. After ½ mile the track nears the A57 road near Cutthroat Bridge. Follow the track as it bears to the left in front of Highshaw Clough. Continue to the left as the path turns up and back across the moorland.

4 Follow the track for 1 mile as it rises steadily across the hillside towards Whinstone Lee Tor. This south-facing hillside is a good place to see and hear the smaller moorland birds.

5 At the junction of tracks and paths where the land drops away ahead take the rocky path uphill to the sharp right bend onto Whinstone Lee Tor. Keep to this path along the edge for about 2^1/$_2$ miles, as it takes a route past a series of intriguingly shaped tors and boulders named on the map as Wheel Stones, White Tor, Salt Cellar, Dovestones Tor, Cakes of Bread. Cross over the junction of paths marked as Bradfield Gate Head and go on to Back Tor. This edge gives great views to the north of the Derwent Reservoirs and surrounding hills, to the east a view over Sheffield; to the west a peek into the u-shaped bowl of Edale and of the Mam Tor - Lose Hill ridge and Win Hill; to the south the gritstone edges of Stanage and Bamford stand out in profile.

6 Immediately before Back Tor (Back Tor wears a trig point - painted white at the time of writing) bear left on the path down hill towards Lost Lad Hillend, south of Greystones Moss (be careful to carry straight on rather than take a left-hand fork before you reach Greystones Moss). After just under 2 miles you emerge in the valley bottom through the Abbey Tip Plantation. This path and track gives a gentle descent across managed moorland and through an area that has been subject to a heather regeneration project.

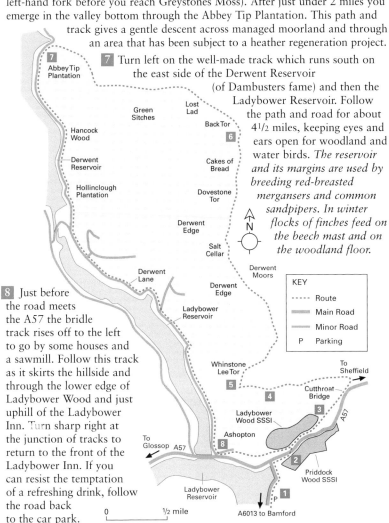

7 Turn left on the well-made track which runs south on the east side of the Derwent Reservoir (of Dambusters fame) and then the Ladybower Reservoir. Follow the path and road for about 4^1/$_2$ miles, keeping eyes and ears open for woodland and water birds. *The reservoir and its margins are used by breeding red-breasted mergansers and common sandpipers. In winter flocks of finches feed on the beech mast and on the woodland floor.*

8 Just before the road meets the A57 the bridle track rises off to the left to go by some houses and a sawmill. Follow this track as it skirts the hillside and through the lower edge of Ladybower Wood and just uphill of the Ladybower Inn. Turn sharp right at the junction of tracks to return to the front of the Ladybower Inn. If you can resist the temptation of a refreshing drink, follow the road back to the car park.

KEY

- - - - Route

▬▬▬ Main Road

▬▬▬ Minor Road

P   Parking

Hillbridge & Park Wood

This woodland valley walk features a wide range of wildlife, including red deer, pied flycatcher and kingfishers. Visit in spring for a fabulous display of bluebells. *By Julia Gow.*

Dipper

START/ PARKING:	Large off-road lay-by on the A5004 (Whaley Bridge to Buxton). On the right 300m after the traffic lights in Whaley Bridge. Grid ref SK 008798.
DISTANCE:	4 miles/6.5km.
DIFFICULTY:	Moderate, some steep sections, muddy underfoot in parts.
OS MAP:	1:50,000 sheet 119 Buxton and Matlock; 1:25,000 Outdoor Leisure 24 White Peak.
TOILETS:	Taxal Church.
PUBLIC TRANSPORT:	Half hourly bus 199 Buxton to Manchester Airport. Disembark on Chapel Road Whaley Bridge. Turn left at the traffic lights, walk up Buxton Road until you reach the lay-by.
LOOK FOR:	Red deer, wood warblers and other woodland birds.
NOTE:	There is no public access to Park Wood.

1 From the lay-by follow the rough track through the wood down to the stream. Cross the stream using the footbridge, or if you are feeling adventurous you could try the ford. Follow the track steeply uphill past Taxal Church.

2 When you reach the road turn left and follow it for about 300 metres. The road soon turns into a track and reaches a gate. Go through the gate and follow the track upwards for approximately 50m until you reach a public foot-path sign on the left. Follow the signed path diagonally across the field on a vague grass track. The footpath can get a little boggy here. *Park Wood, to your left, is the northern section of Hillbridge and Park Wood Nature Reserve. It used to have a shrub layer dominated by rhododendron, but this has nearly been eradicated by Derbyshire Wildlife Trust volunteers. Holly is beginning to replace the rhododendron and the bluebells have started to thrive.*

3 Cross the stile into Hillbridge Wood. *If you are very quiet you may be lucky enough to see some red deer. The birdlife in this woodland is diverse. Nest boxes erected here have resulted in a good population of breeding pied flycatchers.* Follow the footpath through the woodland and into a small meadow. *In the summer you can sit on the bench and enjoy the insect life. As you look towards the River Goyt you may see a dipper, or a flash of blue as a kingfisher flies past.* Leave the nature reserve by the gate and then immediately take the stile on the right. If you do not wish to go further you can cross over the river Goyt and then turn left to follow the footpath through Shallcross Wood and back to the lay-by.

4 Turn right and go over the stile, then bear left towards Knipe. Cross the footbridge. Follow the track climbing diagonally up the hill. Eventually the track goes through a gate, at which point you can see Knipe Farm. Walk up to the farm gate, to the left of the farmhouse.

5 Do not go through the gate into Knipe Farm - walk past it and continue with the dry stone wall immediately on your right. You are now on a concessionary footpath. After about 50m go through the gate in the wall and continue walking in the same southerly direction. Join the track and continue.

6 Eventually, after passing through a gate and over a cattle grid, you will reach Fernilee Reservoir. If you want to extend your walk you can continue along the edge of the reservoir and further up into the Goyt Valley from here.

7 Turn left onto the road that runs along the top of the dam, and at the end of the dam turn left. As the road you are walking on bends to the right, turn immediately left down the road which has a steel barrier across it and runs towards the base of the dam wall. (Be careful not to take the road to the left, a little further round the bend, which also has a steel barrier.) Walk to the end of this road.

8 Follow the footpath with the river on your left and walk through four fields to reach Shallcross Wood. Walk through the wood and at the end turn right up the track and back to the lay-by.

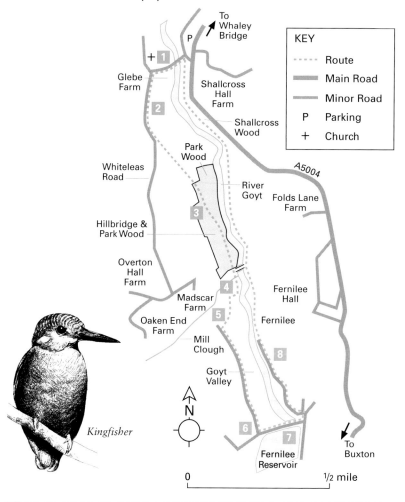

KEY

-----	Route
▨▨▨	Main Road
▬▬▬	Minor Road
P	Parking
+	Church

To Whaley Bridge

Glebe Farm

Shallcross Hall Farm

Shallcross Wood

Park Wood

Whiteleas Road

River Goyt

A5004

Folds Lane Farm

Hillbridge & Park Wood

Overton Hall Farm

Madscar Farm

Fernilee Hall

Oaken End Farm

Fernilee

Mill Clough

Goyt Valley

Kingfisher

N

Fernilee Reservoir

To Buxton

0   1/2 mile

Chee Dale, Deep Dale & Priestcliffe

An excellent walk in spring to see the early wild flowers and trees in blossom. *By Graham and Sonia Brodie.*

START/ PARKING:	Miller's Dale Station car park, off the B6049 near Buxton. Grid ref SK 138732.
DISTANCE:	9 miles/14.5km.
DIFFICULTY:	Steep in places, not suitable for very young children or the elderly. Dales can be muddy and limestone rocky sections slippery. The stepping stones can be covered after heavy rain and this route should not be attempted then. The route crosses the busy A6 twice - please take care.
OS MAP:	1:50,000 sheet 119 Buxton and Matlock; 1:25,000 Outdoor Leisure 24 White Peak.
TOILETS:	At start.
PUBLIC TRANSPORT:	Buses stop on the A6 near the Wye Dale car park (point 3), an alternative start point.
LOOK FOR:	Wild flowers including orchids; butterflies and other invertebrates in summer; dippers along the river.

Nuthatch

1 Walk away from the road out of the west end of the car park by the wide wooden gate and head along the Monsal Trail. Two small paths off to the right take you to Station Quarry in Chee Dale Nature Reserve and to the limekilns, both of which are worth a visit if time allows.

2 Just past the limekilns, take the next path on your right immediately before the viaduct and go down the steep steps into Miller's Dale and the River Wye Valley *(note the fossils on the stone steps)*. Turn right and follow the river to the bridge. Don't cross this bridge, but keeping the river on your left follow this path into Chee Dale, crossing the boardwalks (note the warnings). *Look at still sections of the river, where you may see trout. You may also see dipper, water vole and grey wagtail along the river.* Cross a narrow bridge to the left, where a stream surfaces, heading for Chee Dale. The path eventually goes under overhanging rocks before reaching the first set of stepping stones. Cross the wooden bridge over the river and follow the left bank of the Wye under a viaduct. Ignore a path up steps to the left and follow the sign 'Blackwell Mill'. Cross another bridge onto the right side and continue upstream to the second set of stepping stones. Keeping the river on your left pass under another viaduct, ignoring the steps up to the Monsal Trail. *Look for the yew trees growing out of the rock faces.* At a further viaduct, do not cross the bridge but keep to the path on the right bank and continue until you reach an ivy-clad house with a small private car park. Cross the bridge on the left and follow the road by the river, passing the weir on your right and under three three-arch viaducts until you reach the Wye Dale car park just off the A6.

3 Cross the main road with care to reach the entrance to Topley Pike Quarry. Follow the public footpath to the left of the quarry, keeping the quarry boundary fence on your right. Take a right turn into Deep Dale Nature Reserve, up a steep stepped path and continue along a track by the quicksand pools to a wooden stile and into Deep Dale. *The dale sides are rich in wild flowers, with large areas of bloody cranesbill.* Follow the indistinct rocky path next to a stream in winter.

4 Where you see a stile on your right, turn immediately left to climb the steep zigzag path out of the dale through a flower-rich grassy area which contains clustered bellflower, to the top, a good spot for a picnic. (Before making this ascent you may wish to take a short detour to visit the cave known as Thirst House). The stile in the wall at the top is signed the Midshires Way. This is the start of the walk through open meadows - cross the next four fields in a right (SE) diagonal line using the stone step stiles in the walls until you emerge on a track. Turn left for a few yards to a T junction. Turn right along this track, Caxterway Lane, and follow it to the A5270. Cross the road and follow the sign for the Midshires Way. Pass Shepley Farm on your left, go over a cattle grid and continue into Chelmorton.

5 Turn left up the no through road to the Church Inn. Continue up the hill straight ahead and bear right to a bridleway track that climbs steeply out of the village then through open fields. When the path meets Pillwell Lane turn right for a few yards and then left at a stile. Follow the path until it meets Sough Lane.

6 Turn left and follow the Limestone Way, a walled track that leads down through a gate to the Waterloo Hotel on the A6.

7 Cross the busy A6 onto Priestcliffe Road and continue across the next crossroads, passing Priestcliffe Hall Farm and the 30 mph signs. Ignore the footpath sign on the right and walk ahead to the junction at Lydgate Farm.

8 Turn left down the track, then 100 metres further on take the footpath on your right. Head north east through four fields, then follow the wall. Cross this on stiles with yellow paint markers until you reach the stile which leads into Miller's Dale Quarry Nature Reserve. Turn right by the rusty posts from the old quarry line and follow the path which leads around the rim of the old quarry, through a metal gate and then steeply down a narrow path by the fence. *The base of the old quarry holds a wide range of limestone grassland flowers, including several species of orchid and grass of parnassus in late summer.* Pass a wooden bench and continue down to the stile, which leads back through a short wood and then onto the Monsal Trail. Turn left, past the old limekilns, cross over the viaducts and return to Miller's Dale Station car park.

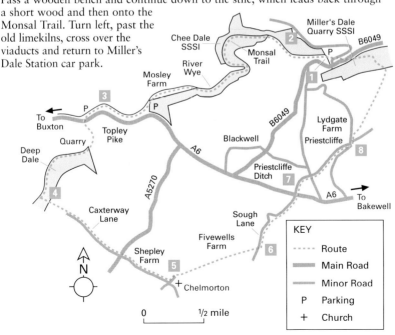

KEY

- - - -	Route
▬▬	Main Road
▬▬	Minor Road
P	Parking
+	Church

Monk's Dale and Chee Dale

This walk takes you to two of the Peak District's best limestone dales, through grassland and woodland, as well as a stretch over farmland with far-reaching views. *By Charles Palmer.*

START/ PARKING: Miller's Dale Station car park, off the B6049 near Tideswell. Grid ref SK 138732.

DISTANCE: 4.6 miles/7.5km.

DIFFICULTY: Many steep ascents and descents. Some sections are very difficult underfoot. Not suitable for small children or people with walking difficulties.

OS MAP: 1:50,000 sheet 119 Buxton and Matlock; 1:25,000 Outdoor Leisure 24 White Peak.

TOILETS: At start.

PUBLIC TRANSPORT: TM Travel operates a Sunday service from Buxton.

Water Vole

LOOK FOR: Orchids on the quarry floor in summer; variety of wildflowers throughout spring and summer; ravens.

1 From the car park, with the building behind you, turn left (east) on the Monsal Trail and cross the viaduct over the river. On your right you pass the old lime kilns - the interpretation boards make interesting reading. After about 400 metres take the path down to the left, signposted 'Public Footpath to Miller's Dale'. The path now drops steeply to the river. *In spring look out for wood anemones and butterbur.*

2 Cross the river on the footbridge and turn left onto a lane. Almost immediately, cross the B6049 and take the footpath to the left of the church. Climb the path and, once through the gate at the top, go straight on (don't turn left). Now you enter Monk's Dale National Nature Reserve. Cross a footbridge after about 500 metres and follow the valley bottom, first through grassland and then down a steep rocky path through a wood, before emerging onto grazed farmland.

Bee Orchid

3 The path now leaves the grassy slopes and enters a wood. Please note that the track is very uneven here. *Early in the year, the dense carpets of vivid green plants close to the ground in wet areas are golden saxifrage. Later in the year you'll see the drooping yellow and mauve flowers of water avens.*

4 Shortly after emerging from the wood in Monk's Dale you'll see a lane in front of you. Before you reach it, bear left around the side of the hill and you'll soon find a path heading steeply up the field. Pass through a gate onto a path that runs between a pair of dry stone walls. You now reach the highest point of the walk. There is a fine view of Miller's Dale Nature Reserve to your left, and in the far distance the moors behind Chatsworth. Immediately after passing through a gate you'll see a gap in the wall on your left. Go through the wall and on through three or four fields towards the hamlet of Wormhill.

5 When you reach the farmyard at Wormhill turn left at the junction of three paths, then right between two houses and onto the road. Go past the church on your left. At the road junction turn left and walk downhill. Just before the road reaches its lowest point, turn right at the signpost to Chee Dale and Blackwell.

6 This path soon leads through a gate into Chee Dale Nature Reserve. Don't take the path that drops steeply to your right, but veer gently to the left instead. When you emerge into an open grassed area the path turns left. At the bottom of the descent go straight on (carefully!) to the edge of the dale, for a spectacular view of Chee Dale. *The thin soils on the steep limestone banks in front of you support a rich selection of lime-loving plants. In early June it is carpeted with the unusually hairy kidney vetch and later with the delicate flowers of rock rose.* The path now drops gradually down the side of the dale, through a gate to the river.

7 A shorter alternative route is to cross the bridge and turn left, walk up the field through a gate and left onto the Monsal Trail which will return you to the car park. Stay on the left bank of the river and follow it as it winds down towards the road beneath the station. *If you stay on the river side and look carefully you are almost certain to see a dipper, and if you are lucky a water vole.*

8 Just before you reach the road turn left and climb up to the old station platforms to finish your walk.

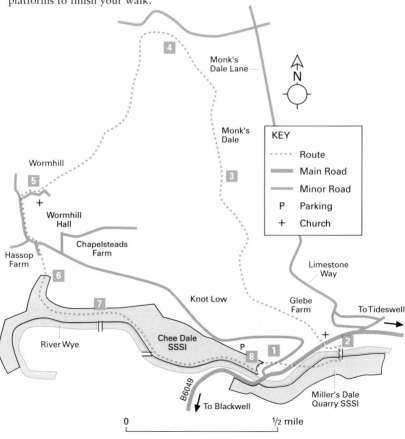

Priestcliffe Lees

A challenging route with rich rewards, especially in spring and summer when wildflowers abound. *By Ian and Sue Weatherley.*

START/ PARKING:	Tideswell Dale car park. Grid ref SK 154742. Parking charge.
DISTANCE:	9½ miles/15km.
DIFFICULTY:	A long walk with some steep climbs and steps.
OS MAP:	1:50,000 sheet 119, Buxton and Matlock; 1:25,000 Outdoor Leisure 24 White Peak.
TOILETS:	At start and Monsal Head.
PUBLIC TRANSPORT:	T M Travel Service 65 from Buxton stops at Tideswell Dale.
LOOK FOR:	Limestone flowers and plants, lead mining landscape, industrial architecture.

Fragrant Orchid

1 Go past the toilets down the dale. At the first fork go left to see the sculptures, then follow the path to the Litton Mill road. *In April coltsfoot and lesser celandine can be seen by the stream and wood anemone flowers among the trees.*

2 Turn left and follow the road to the edge of Litton Mill hamlet. Turn right, signposted Monsal Trail and cross the bridge over the River Wye. Climb the steps and steep path up to the old railway line, the Monsal Trail. Turn right and follow the trail under a bridge. *There are cowslips, anemones, orpine and valerian beside the trail.* After just over ½ mile you reach a path crossing the trail and a large bench.

3 Turn left, past a Derbyshire Wildlife Trust interpretation board for Priestcliffe Lees Nature Reserve, and climb steeply through the ash and hazel woodland. After a stile you come out onto open grassland. Towards the top of the dale side you reach a wall corner by a farm and a footpath sign. Keep the farm immediately on your left and go through a stile onto a track by a Derbyshire Wildlife Trust sign. *Note the old spoil heaps that are rich in limestone plants such as salad burnet, orchids and mountain pansy.*

4 When you reach a T-junction by the New Barn - a rather elderly looking building - turn left.

5 Continue for about another ½ mile to a sharp right hand bend in the track with a Derbyshire Wildlife Trust sign ahead. *A diversion into the reserve will take you across some old lead spoil heaps rich in mountain pansy and spring sandwort.* When you rejoin the track, note the capped mineshaft on the left.

6 Look south across High Dale to the maze of drystone walls. Continue to a copse and a gate leading past Top Farm, Brushfield. Follow the track past the farm, through a second gate and descend to some newly renovated cottages. Turn left at the signpost through the gate marked "5mph children playing", walk in front of the cottages and out through a second gate. Take the right fork just through the gate. You are now above Taddington Dale and the A6, although it is difficult to see, even in winter.

7 When you reach a copse and a gate, go up the slope to an ash tree and wall. Take the left fork. The track can be muddy and rutted to the next wall, gate and stile. You follow the track above Monsal Dale with good views of Fin Cop, an ancient settlement, and Hob's House, an impressive land-slip. *Note the fossils in the wall.*

8 After a short distance you see a large dew pond on the left. Start to descend, enjoying the good views of Monsal Head. The track is rough and stony here. When it turns sharp left go straight on down the marked bridleway. This leads to the end of the Monsal Viaduct. Turn right onto the viaduct for views of the dale and an interpretation board. Go back across the viaduct and follow the trail past Monsal Dale station to the end of the trail for this section. If you need a toilet break, leave the viaduct and go up the path to the Monsal Head Hotel, where they are signposted.

9 Go through the gate and follow the path across the hillside to the steps down to the millpond supplying Cressbrook Mill. Cross the bridge into the mill complex. There is a weekend 'brew stop' in the folly but no toilets. At the road turn left. Take the right fork in the road and climb steadily. The road is usually quiet but needs care. Further along the road, take a right fork signed 'Ravensdale, no through road'. Follow this to the cottages.

10 Go past the cottages, through damp woodland full of ramsons and wood anemone, to a nature reserve sign and bridge. *Just over the bridge is bird cherry and a meadow on the right rich in limestone flowers.* Take the right hand fork in the path and climb steadily. You emerge onto open grassland with some scrub and a wall corner at a high point. Descend, bearing left to some stepping stones.

11 Cross the stepping stones, go through the gate and into Tansley Dale. *You may see wheatear here.* Continue up the dale to a stile. Cross this and bear right to a wall corner and on to a second stile and track. Turn left onto the track and follow it to a road. Turn left and follow the road to a left bend. Go straight on through a stile. Cross three more stiles and bear left onto a narrow fenced path to a lane. Cross this and descend to the road.

12 Turn left and take the tarmac pavement to the main road. Turn left and immediately go through a gate on the left. This takes you onto a concession path leading back to the car park.

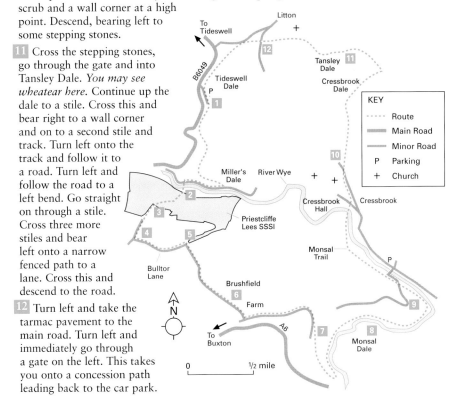

Hartington Meadows

A moderate walk in the White Peak plateau lands offering flowers, birds, ferns and distant views. Spring and summer are the best times to appreciate the flowers but there is enjoyment to be had all year round. *By Steve Price.*

START/
PARKING: Pay and display car park at the old Hartington Station, off the B5054 road to Hartington from the A515. Grid ref SK 150 611.

DISTANCE: 4 miles/6.5km.

DIFFICULTY: Easy.

OS MAP: 1:50,000 sheet 119 Buxton and Matlock; 1:25,000 Outdoor Leisure 24 White Peak.

TOILETS: In car park.

PUBLIC
TRANSPORT: Infrequent Buxton - Ashbourne buses stop on the A515 (Jug and Glass Inn), 1km from the start point.

LOOK FOR: A range of wildflowers in spring and summer.

Fragrant
Orchid

1 Leave the car park from the opposite end to the entrance road, keeping the toilet block on your right and go south on the Tissington Trail for 50 metres.

2 Follow a public footpath off to the left, up steps over a wall by a stone ladder stile and follow the footpath ahead across old limestone quarry spoil heaps, on which many colonising species of flowers are to be found (limestone flowers) to enter a field by a small gate.

3 The footpath cuts diagonally to the left and enters the Hartington Meadows Nature Reserve by way of a stile and wicket gate.

4 Follow the footpath up the right hand side of the field and after 50 metres go through a wicket gate, *taking some time to appreciate the flowers and delicate grasses here.* Continue on the path which sticks close to the dry stone wall on your right. At the top of the slope, before the path swings off to the left, look over to the right to see the old silica sand pits. *Sands and clays were extracted from here last century and used to make refractory bricks to line the kilns associated with the limestone quarries. These pocket deposits of sand and clay are about 6 million years old and formed in solution hollows in the underlying limestone which itself was formed over 300 million years ago when this area was covered in shallow tropical seas. Listen out for the deep 'cronk-cronk' of ravens that nest in the quarries nearby.*

5 Continue to follow the public footpath which turns left and goes through a wicket gate and takes you into the hay meadows. *In June the meadows support a wider range of grassland flowers.* (Note: if you go straight ahead rather than turning left you will find yourself on the Hartington Meadows short walk signposted Wildlife Walk). *Please keep to the path, hay is a valuable crop for farmers and is easily damaged by trampling. Listen for skylarks singing.*

6 Go straight ahead on the path which again follows the field boundary to join the road from the A515 to Hartington.

7 Turn left, cross the road onto the opposite verge and, minding the traffic, follow the road for 75 metres to take the lane on the right.

8 Follow the lane, *noting the heather, bilberry and gorse - acid-loving plants which grow well here because the heavy rainfall has leached the calcium out of the soil.*

9 At the top of the rise look ahead to the left to see the mound of the Arbor Low tumulus. Straight on are views of the gritstone landscape of East Moor behind the Chatsworth Estate.

10 Cross the A515 to continue on the track opposite and after 500 metres turn left onto the High Peak Trail & Pennine Bridleway. *Note the wind break strips of planted woodland which are a feature of the limestone plateau.*

11 After the trail goes under a bridge it enters a cutting. *Start to look for ferns growing out of the rocky sides, look particularly on the shady north side.*

12 The trail goes under the road bridge for the A515, note the age of the bridge and the width left for the road even at that time. As you pass under the bridge look up to see the ornate inscriptions on both faces of the bridge.

13 As the trail comes out of the cutting and swings to the right views open out of the upper valley of the River Dove over to the western moorlands of Axe Edge.

14 Turn sharp left onto the Tissington Trail which returns you after 2 miles to the starting point. This section of the walk takes you through one deep cutting and three shallower cuttings and views are offered of the limestone landscape over to the Staffordshire hills. *Look out for a range of flowers, including orchids, on the trailside.*

15 *Just before crossing the bridge returning to the start point look to the left to the disused quarry where the bedding of the limestone is well displayed.*

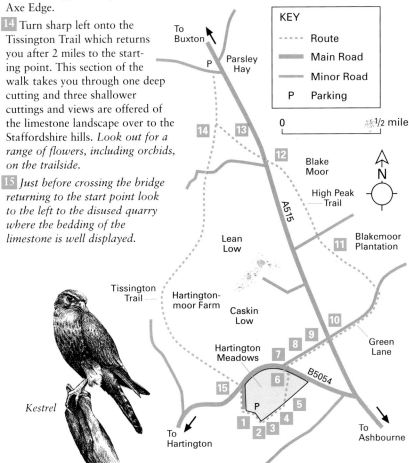

KEY

- - - -	Route
▬▬▬	Main Road
▬▬▬	Minor Road
P	Parking

0   1/2 mile

To Buxton

Parsley Hay

Blake Moor

High Peak Trail

A515

Blakemoor Plantation

Lean Low

Tissington Trail

Hartington-moor Farm

Caskin Low

Hartington Meadows

Green Lane

B5054

Kestrel

To Hartington

To Ashbourne

N

Hartington Meadows

A short alternative to the previous walk for those with less time or energy.
By Steve Price.

START/ PARKING:	Pay and display car park at the old Hartington Station, off the B5054 road to Hartington from the A515. Grid ref SK 150 611.
DISTANCE:	1¹/₂ miles/2.5 km.
DIFFICULTY:	Easy.
OS MAP:	1:50,000 sheet 119 Buxton and Matlock; 1:25,000 Outdoor Leisure 24 White Peak.
TOILETS:	At the car park.
PUBLIC TRANSPORT:	Infrequent Buxton - Ashbourne buses stop on the A515 (Jug and Glass Inn), 1km from the start point.
LOOK FOR:	Wildflowers in summer; ravens, skylarks.

Small Copper Butterfly

1 Leave the car park from the opposite end to the entrance road, to go south on the Tissington Trail for 50m.

2 Follow a public footpath off to the left, up steps over a wall by a stile and follow the footpath ahead across old limestone quarry spoil heaps to enter a field.

3 The footpath cuts diagonally to the left and enters the Hartington Meadows Nature Reserve by way of a stile and wicket gate.

4 Follow the footpath up the right hand side of the field and after 50m go through a wicket gate, taking some time to appreciate the flowers and delicate grasses here. Continue on the path which sticks close to the dry stone wall. At the top of the slope, before the path swings off to the left, look over to the right to see the old silica sand pits. *Sands and clays were extracted from here last century and used to make refractory bricks to line the kilns associated with the limestone quarries. These pocket deposits of sand and clay are about 6 million years old and formed in solution hollows in the underlying limestone which itself was formed over 300 million years ago when this area was covered in shallow tropical seas. Listen out for the deep 'cronk-cronk' of ravens that nest in the quarries nearby.* Go straight ahead following a concessionary way-marked path through a wicket gate to follow a route between two drystone walls. *(Note: if you follow the public footpath to the left rather than go straight ahead you will find yourself on the Hartington Meadows long walk).*

5 Follow the path which takes you across the grassland with the silica sand pit on your right. Do not venture into the sand pit - the sands are deep and soft.

6 Leave the nature reserve onto the narrow Heathcote Lane. Turn right and follow this lane for about 1km until the road bridge across the Tissington Trail.

7 Take the footpath to the left just before the bridge to join the trail.

8 Turn right on the trail which takes you back to the start point after 750m.

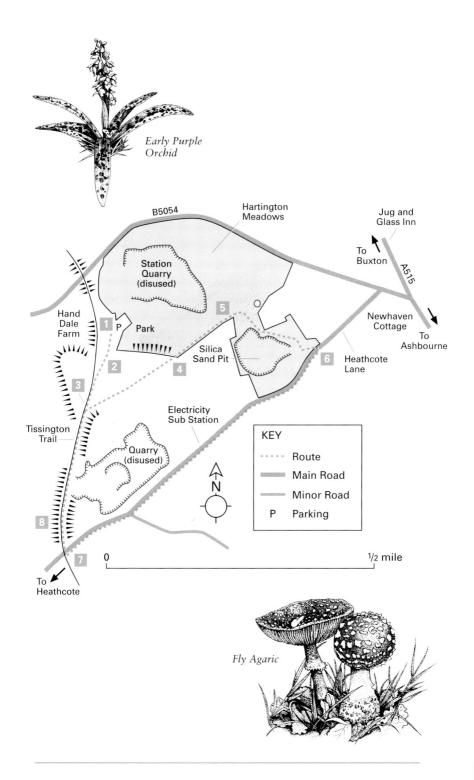

Early Purple
Orchid

B5054

Hartington
Meadows

Jug and
Glass Inn

To
Buxton

A515

Station
Quarry
(disused)

5

Hand
Dale
Farm

1 P

Park

Newhaven
Cottage

To
Ashbourne

2

4

Silica
Sand Pit

6

Heathcote
Lane

3

Tissington
Trail

Electricity
Sub Station

Quarry
(disused)

KEY

Route

Main Road

Minor Road

P   Parking

N

8

0

1/2 mile

7

To
Heathcote

Fly Agaric

Hollinhill & Markland Grips

This route has all-year-round interest, with spectacular magnesian limestone cliffs in the section passing through the nature reserve. *By Jim Russell.*

START/ PARKING:	Park at entrance to Ringer Lane, Elmton, next to the pump and village interpretation board; downhill from the church. Grid ref SK 503735.
DISTANCE:	Approximately 5 miles/8km.
DIFFICULTY:	Lane, footpath and roadside walking. May be muddy.
OS MAP:	1:50,000 120 Mansfield and Worksop; 1:25,000 Explorer 269 Chesterfield and Alfreton.
TOILETS:	None on route.
PUBLIC TRANSPORT:	No bus services to Elmton.
LOOK FOR:	Variety of birdlife all year round; orchids and other flowering plants.

Great Spotted Woodpecker

1 Walk up the lane, past the cottage and turn left onto Oxcroft Lane. Continue to the junction with Border Lane, where an old disused quarry is on the left. *The hedges contain a good variety of species, including spindle, field maple and dogwood. Also present are mature ash and holly trees. Corn buntings and common whitethroats can be heard or seen in spring and summer, as can common and red-legged partridges, and even the occasional quail has been heard calling.*

2 Turn right onto Border Lane and continue down for 1½ miles. *The grass verges are rich in plant life such as greater stitchwort and knapweed, which attract butterflies including gatekeepers and skippers. Birds to look for include yellowhammers, linnets and tree sparrows. Where it meets Ringer Lane, a stream goes underneath before flowing into Markland Grips and onto Cresswell Crags.* (NB: for a shorter route, from the starting point, continue along Ringer Lane, then turn right onto Border Lane).

3 At the end of Border Lane, turn right then cross the road to the stile opposite. Take the footpath bearing right across a meadow, with Markland Farm to the right, then continue down a farm track. At the end of the track, turn right onto a disused railway line for a short distance. *This stretch is notable for plants such as greater knapweed and mignonette. The site of an Iron Age fort can also be seen on farmland across the railway.* Take the signposted footpath off to the right of the disused railway line. The path then descends into Markland Grips through a grassland area, *where flowers such as kidney vetch, wild thyme and rock rose grow.* Go over the stile and turn left under the old railway bridge.

Speckled Wood Butterfly

4 Turn right, go over the stile beside the nature reserve sign, and follow the path, initially along the side of the stream, and then continuing through the magnesian limestone gorge, until you reach Upper Mill Farm, turning left just before joining the lane. *The magnesian limestone cliffs get higher as the path winds through the Grips and while ash is the commonest tree, large-leaved limes and yew trees also grow on the cliffs. Look for hart's tongue fern as well. Spotted flycatchers, chiffchaffs and blackcaps can be seen in summer, whilst fieldfares, grey wagtails and kingfishers are present in the winter months. Bullfinches, nuthatches and goldcrests can be seen throughout the year. Speckled wood and holly blue butterflies occur in this area.*

5 Turn right, past the farm buildings and proceed towards Hazelmere Road. *Look for purging buckthorn trees on the laneside.*

6 Turn right at the lane end onto Hazelmere Road. *As you approach Elmton village, there is a wide grass verge on the left. This has received recognition for the plants that grow on it, including bee orchids and sedges. The road swings to the right and the Elmtree pub is on the left. It's worth a visit for a drink or a meal, after which the car park is down the road to the left of the church.*

To avoid walking on the road, you could turn right at the footpath sign, passing through three fields onto a lane with a wall on the right. Turn left at the end of the lane, then right at the junction beside the church and downhill to return to the start.

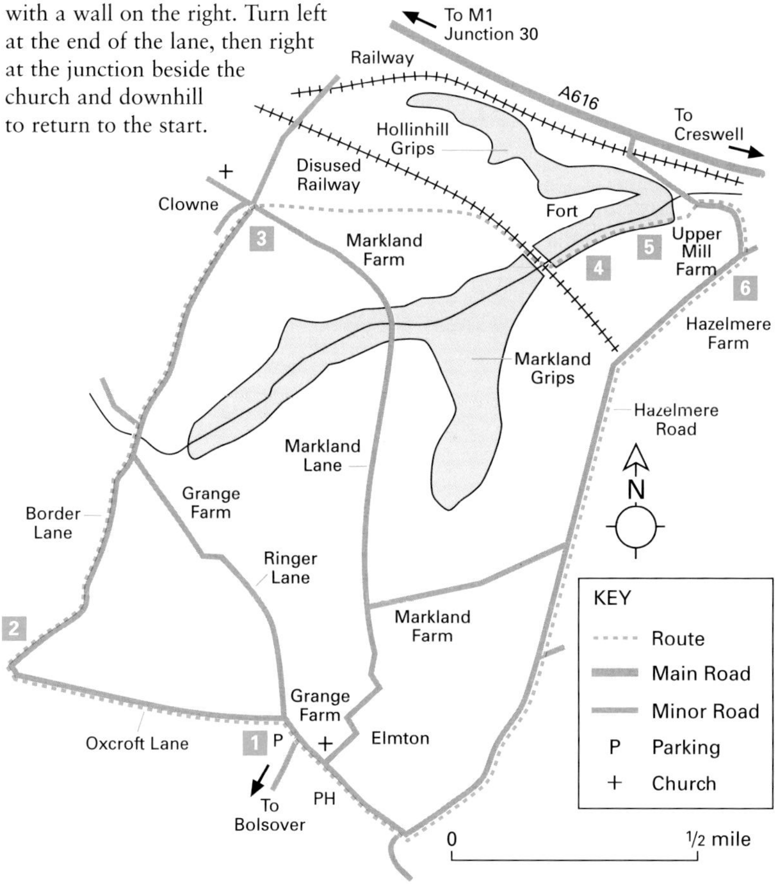

KEY

- - - -	Route
▬▬▬	Main Road
▬▬▬	Minor Road
P	Parking
+	Church

0   ½ mile

Carr Vale

A short walk for all seasons. *By Steve Price.*

START/ PARKING:	The car park for the Derbyshire County Council Peter Fidler Reserve/Stockley Trail at the end of Riverside Way. Turn south for 150m off the A632 at a roundabout at the bottom of Station Road (Bolsover Hill), signed Gateway Business Park. Grid ref SK 461 706.
DISTANCE:	1¹/₂ miles/2.5km.
DIFFICULTY:	Easy, a level walk mostly on surfaced paths. There is wheelchair access for the outward half of the walk.
OS MAP:	1:50,000 sheet 120 Mansfield & Worksop; 1:25,000 sheet 269 Chesterfield & Alfreton.
TOILETS:	Bolsover, on Cavendish Walk (from car park behind shops).
PUBLIC TRANSPORT:	Bolsover - Chesterfield buses stop on the A632, 150m from the start point.
LOOK FOR:	Winter wildfowl, hares, dragonflies and breeding birds in summer.

Great Crested Newt

1 The car park is adjacent to the trails around the Peter Fidler Reserve. From the car park, go through the squeeze stile by the entrance gate to the carpark which takes you onto the trail by the Stockley Trail interpretation board. Continue on the trail past the interpretation board. After 100 metres the trail crosses the River Doe Lea - take the trail to the left through a stile.

2 The monument on the right is in celebration of Peter Fidler - read about him here. *Keep an ear open for skylarks singing high in the air.*

3 Continue on the path above the old colliery ponds to the left.

4 As the path cuts back right, away from the ponds, a 50 metre detour to the left gives you a closer look at the ponds. *They are alive with dragonflies in the summer and with luck you may glimpse a water vole.*

5 On joining another trail at a T-junction turn left and continue for 200 metres as the trail rises over an old railway embankment (ignore the first path off to the left) to reach a Derbyshire Wildlife Trust interpretation board for Carr Vale Nature Reserve.

6 Turn left in front of the interpretation board and field gate to follow the path into the reserve.

7 Follow the path alongside the banks of the main pond, taking the right-hand path which turns right after 50 metres to keep between the pond and the river (ignore the path which goes straight ahead over the river). *In winter a range of diving duck, including pochard and tufted duck can be seen. In spring look out for the mating 'dances' of the great crested grebe.*

8 Continue ahead on the reserve path paying a visit to the 'Mound' and 'Lapwing Lookout' viewing screens along the way. *From these a good range of wildfoul, waders and reedbed and marsh birds may be seen at most times of the year.*

9 Leave the nature reserve through a squeeze stile and over a small footbridge onto a concession path over a farm field.

10 After 150 metres take a public footpath to the left over a footbridge for 100 metres to join the Stockley Trail.

11 Turn left on the Stockley Trail and follow this for 1km to return to the car park with a lovely view of Bolsover Castle on the hill to the right. *Look for hedgerow birds and finches on the trail.*

12 Optional extra - the Snipe Bog reserve. Walk away from the car park, cross the busy A632 and follow the sign for the 'Snipe Bog Reserve'.

An out-and-back walk of 400 metres will let you explore this small diverse area of pools and woodland.

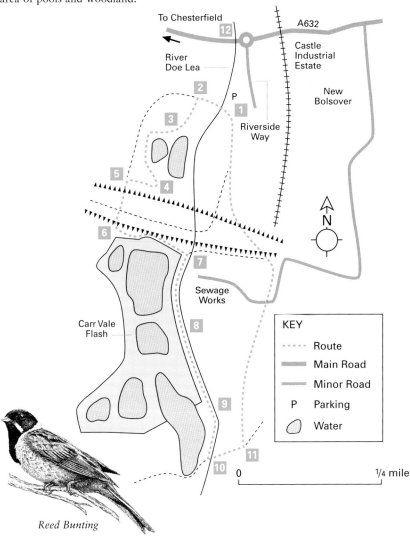

Reed Bunting

Erewash Meadows

Enjoy watching birds in winter and butterflies and dragonflies in summer on this walk at the border with Nottinghamshire. *By Dave Sneap.*

START/ PARKING:	Stoneyford Lodge Inn. Boat Lane, above the Stoneyford Lodge Inn. Grid ref SK 444 494.
DISTANCE:	1¹/₂ miles - 3¹/₂ miles/2.5km - 5.5km.
DIFFICULTY:	An easy-going walk but can be overgrown in summer and muddy in winter.
OS MAP:	1:50,000 sheet 120 Mansfield & Worksop; 1:50,000 sheet 129 Nottingham and Loughborough.
TOILETS:	None on route - toilets at the Stoneyford Lodge Inn for customers.
PUBLIC TRANSPORT:	Service 1 Trent Barton from Eastwood, Nottingham stops in nearby Brinsley and Jacksdale.
LOOK FOR:	Wildfowl, wading birds, great crested and little grebe, water voles.

Lapwing

1   From the Stoneyford Lodge Inn go down the road over the railway bridge, passing the Kennels on your left, cross the stile and turn immediately left to a second stile leading into Big Marsh meadow. Below and to your right is Kennels Flash, a shallow scrape dammed to control the water level.
When conditions are right, it is worth checking for waders. Keep dogs on leads and stay close to the left-hand hedgerow to avoid disturbing any birds.

2   Walk along the path, over two more stiles to arrive at a large isolated post on a rise. *Look for great crested and little grebes and various species of duck in winter.* From here you can continue straight ahead past the Erewash Meadows Nature Reserve until you cross a stile just before reaching the canal (point 4); or you can take an interesting detour off to your left. For the alternative route, go over the stile to your left, leading to a path (which can be overgrown in summer) alongside a remnant of the old canal. *It takes you through an area of willow and hawthorn to a clearing that is good for butterflies in the summer.* Follow the path through the 'hills and holes' and into the Top Copse, a small area of derelict woodland.

3   On reaching the fence line, turn to your right over the footbridge at the end of the canal.

4   *A cautious approach here and you may see water shrew in the clear water just above the meter sluice.* Head for the left-hand side of the embankment and the old brick supports and up the steps onto the embankment. About half way along the top is a lookout point (a bench seat that looks over Big Marsh). Continuing along the top, go down the steps to the River Erewash, *looking for water voles as you approach the footbridge over the river.* Once over the bridge, follow the path across the middle of the field until it joins the farm track with Bagthorpe Brook appearing on your left.

5   After about 150 metres, turn right up a narrow path, signposted Brinsley Gin, which rises across the fields. Follow this path, firstly to the left of the hedge, then crossing over a stile which takes you onto a trackway to the right of the hedge, for ³/4 mile over the high fields, *where brown hare, grey and red legged partridge, lapwing and skylark are seen.*

6 At Gin Farm, pass to the right of farm buildings and continue round to the right, passing Ladywood Shooting Club car park, also on your right, to the gateway and clapper gate directly ahead. This short length of farm track beyond the gate leads to a second gateway and clapper gate and then a footpath through the field to the river. Before reaching the footbridge over the river, the path passes the river bank on a bend. *Pause here to look for water voles. This is also a good spot for kingfisher and grey wagtail.*

7 On crossing the footbridge, the Kennels and the roadway back to the Stoneyford Lodge Inn are ahead and slightly to your right. To continue your walk through the southern part of the reserve, turn left after crossing the river and follow the path alongside the river. Cross two stiles then look for the gate and stile entrance to Railway Marsh, which lies slightly to the right.

8 *The areas of water on this marsh can be difficult to see, but just through the gate is an area of slightly higher ground, so scan from here to see what wildfowl are about. When water levels are low, waders occur, mainly snipe and green sandpiper, but other species have also been seen, including spoonbill and little egret. In winter, cormorants sit in the dead riverside trees, joining the resident grey herons. In autumn, the field to your right below the railway embankment, is often covered in thistles which attract goldfinches. There is a small shallow pool as you near the railway bridge that has little grebe and ruddy duck and also holds a colony of great crested newts.*

9 Cross the front of the railway bridge and go over a stile onto the footpath beside the railway embankment.

10 On approaching the A610 road bridge over Plumptre Road, which is now in front of you, turn left down the farm track to the causeway over the river. Note that the causeway is under water when the river is high and is sometimes impassable. *This is one of the best places to see water rail, especially in winter when they sometimes cross the causeway. At the end of the causeway, just after the road starts to rise, there is a winter bird feeding station on the left.*

11 Just past the fence line on the left, cross the stile into the field, signposted Brinsley Hill and Jacksdale and pass behind a small triangular copse. As the view to your left opens out, Spoonbill Pool can be seen and as this area holds most of the wild-fowl it is worth stopping for a few minutes. *During the winter, 200-300 mixed duck species occur, mainly teal and wigeon.* Continue along the footpath and over two more stiles to Taylors Pond and Marsh. This is a small overgrown field with a small pond heavily fringed by reed mace. *Stonechats are often seen here in autumn and the field is good for flowers and butter-flies in summer.* Keep to the path as it follows the hedge-row and then curves left to the footbridge over the river.

12 Turn right over the bridge and follow the path back to the Kennels and Stoneyford Lodge Inn.

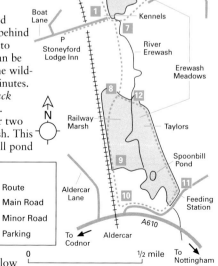

Big
Marsh

Boat
Lane

Kennels

P

Stoneyford
Lodge Inn

River
Erewash

Erewash
Meadows

Railway
Marsh

Taylors

Spoonbill
Pond

N

KEY

----- Route

Main Road

Minor Road

P   Parking

Aldercar
Lane

Feeding
Station

A610

To
Codnor

To   Aldercar

0   1/2 mile

To
Nottingham

Rose End Meadows & Gang Mine

Two of the Trust's grassland reserves, rich in wildflowers through spring
and summer, provide the setting for this scenic walk. *By Paul Robinson.*

START/ PARKING:	National Stone Centre. Grid ref SK 285553.
DISTANCE:	6 miles/9.6km.
DIFFICULTY:	Some steep ascents and descents.
OS MAP:	1:50,000 sheet 119 Buxton and Matlock; 1:25,000 Outdoor Leisure 24 White Peak.
TOILETS:	National Stone Centre, Middleton Top Visitor Centre.
PUBLIC TRANSPORT:	Trent Barton service R61 Derby - Bakewell stops at Porter Lane and Middleton at the entrance to the National Stone Centre. For more information contact Traveline on 0870 608 2 608.
LOOK FOR:	Wildflowers in spring and summer; great crested newts in the dewponds in spring.

Wood Anemone

1 Leaving the car park on the right, a track ascends slightly to join the High
Peak Trail. Turn right and follow the former railway line uphill for just over
1¹/2 miles to Middleton Top Engine House. The old embankments are a refuge
for many plants. About half way up the incline, the trail passes under a former
mineral line viaduct before entering a man-made gorge where cliffs rise up on
either side. At the top of the incline, go through a gate before passing the
engine house on your left.

2 Just before the cycle hire centre, leave the trail by the steps on your right,
signed to Middleton Moor. Follow the fence around to the right through the
gate before turning left up a wide track past two groups of large limestone
boulders. Follow the track straight ahead, across Middleton Moor, to a stile
where you turn right on to a walled track. The lane soon bears left, before
descending to a T junction. Turn right, down the road, towards the centre of
Middleton village.

3 Cross the road to Duke Street and follow it to the end where a walled lane
begins. On reaching a group of smallholders' barns the lane forks both left and
right. Keep to the track straight ahead of you. Continue down this walled track
until you reach a gate with a narrow squeeze stile on the right, just past a
dewpond. A grassy path now heads downhill into a small valley, which narrows
into a walled path before reaching a wooden stile. Climb this to enter the
woodland. The path winds downhill, passing Groaning Torr on your left before
descending steeply through Slinter Wood. Leave the woodland through the next
gate, taking the higher path across the field.

4 The path heads round to the right, towards a gate, with a wooden gate on
the right. Go through this but ignore the next gate almost immediately on your
right and head down the small path with the woodland fence on your right.
The path heads round to the right and straight ahead is a stone stile through
which you pass back into Slinter Wood.

5 Go through the stile, heading downhill towards Slinter Wood cottage on your left. Continue on the path through the wood with the brook and old disused millponds on your left. The path gradually bends right along a raised terrace heading for Cromford. Ignore the steps on the left down to the old mill and continue along the main path. It climbs uphill before passing a small cliff face on your right, then descends to join another path directly ahead. Turn right uphill towards the council house estate above and right again at the top of the rise on to Alabaster Lane.

6 Ascend the lane with the houses on your left, over a road and up past a gate with the DWT reserve sign on it to the second stile, approximately 100 metres on your left. Go over the stile and follow the path up the slope across Rose End Meadows Nature Reserve. *The grassland flowers of this area are rich and varied throughout the spring and summer.* Where the path forks take the right hand path past an area of scrub and out onto open grassland again. *In the next field you pass a restored dewpond, where great crested newts breed.* Keep straight ahead through the third field, passing through the old gritstone gateposts overhung by a large, old hazel tree. Head down to the kissing gate on your right. This leads out of the reserve, down a path with the steep sides of a large old spoil heap on your right.

7 Turn left at the bottom of this slope, then right along a track about 25 metres further down. Follow this track, with gardens on your left and take the next track right, leading slightly uphill towards the quarry works. Cross the road immediately in front of you and turn left on to the walled path. 50 metres up on your right take the green waymarked footpath, climbing up steps at first, before skirting the edge of the quarry. Keep to the well-marked path around the quarry edge.

8 Continue past the far end of the quarry and after 200 metres take the path off left through the kissing gate to enter the reserve. *The lead-tolerant plants, spring sandwort and alpine pennycress grow on the lead spoil heaps in spring and summer. The reserve is also a good place to see a range of butterflies.* Turn right at the T junction (with an old barn on the left) to join a public path, and another restored dewpond appears on your left. Continue alongside the fence to the next gate, through which you meet an unmetalled lane, heading towards a small bridge on the left. Go over the bridge towards the road ahead, crossing it to enter the Stone Centre car park on your left.

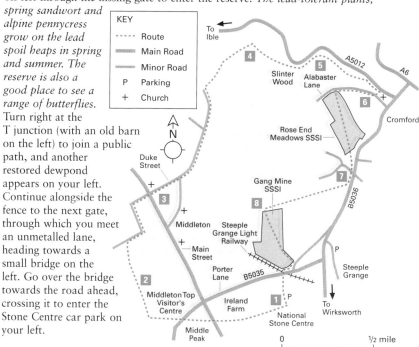

KEY

- - - - - Route
▬▬▬▬ Main Road
▬▬▬▬ Minor Road
P   Parking
+   Church

Derwentside & Cromford Canal

An easy-going linear walk along the Cromford Canal, ideal for a spring or summer's day. *By Gordon Swain.*

START/ PARKING:	Cromford Wharf. Grid ref SK 299571.
DISTANCE:	5 miles/8km.
DIFFICULTY:	Easy, canal towpath - may be muddy.
OS MAP:	1:50,000 sheet 119 Buxton and Matlock.
TOILETS:	Cromford Wharf and High Peak Junction.
PUBLIC TRANSPORT:	Railway station at Cromford, buses stop on the A6, both within easy walking distance of the start. For more information contact Traveline on 0870 608 2 608.
LOOK FOR:	Water voles; frogs and toads; grass snakes; dragonflies and damselflies; orange tip and brimstone butterflies; dippers in the River Derwent.

Little Grebe

1 From Cromford Wharf head south-east along the canal towpath. *This is a good place to see little grebe as they continually submerge in search of food.*

2 *High Peak Junction was the point where freight transferred from the canal and the railway to the High Peak Railway, via a pulley system up the Sheep Pasture Incline.* At the Junction cross the canal over the turntable bridge and continue along the footpath to the right of the canal, taking the left fork after passing the canalside buildings. *The building to your left on the opposite side of the canal is the Leawood Pumphouse, which was constructed to pump water from the river into the canal. It has been restored and is open to the public on certain weekends when the engine is in steam.* Continue along the canalside, passing over the aqueduct taking the canal over the River Derwent.

3 Immediately after crossing the aqueduct on the opposite side of the canal is the ruin of the lock keeper's cottage, where the Leawood arm splits off from the main canal and heads towards Smedley's Mill at Lea. Do not cross the canal by the footbridge but continue along the main canal path, and Derwentside Nature Reserve now appears on the right. *Look for wild daffodils here in spring.* The reserve ends at Gregory's Tunnel where there is a footpath to Homesford to the right and, on top of the tunnel, a footpath to Holloway to the left. *Singing pied flycatcher can be heard in the wood on both sides of the canal.*

4 Access through the tunnel can be a little damp at times and is difficult for wheelchairs. A steep footpath goes over the tunnel. *The turning circle at the south end of the tunnel is a good place to see both little grebe and water vole.* Proceed along the towpath to Whatstandwell, passing the hamlet of Robin Hood to the left. After passing under the B5035 you reach the Trust's Cromford Canal Nature Reserve - *another good location to see water vole -* which you follow for two miles to Ambergate. The reserve ends at the bridge with the Wildlife Trust information sign in front of it.

5 Leave the canal by the stile to the right of the bridge and go down the metalled road to the A6. Almost immediately opposite the end of the road is the bus stop where you can get a bus back to Cromford. By turning left and walking towards Ambergate you will see signs to the railway station, from where you can get a train to Cromford.

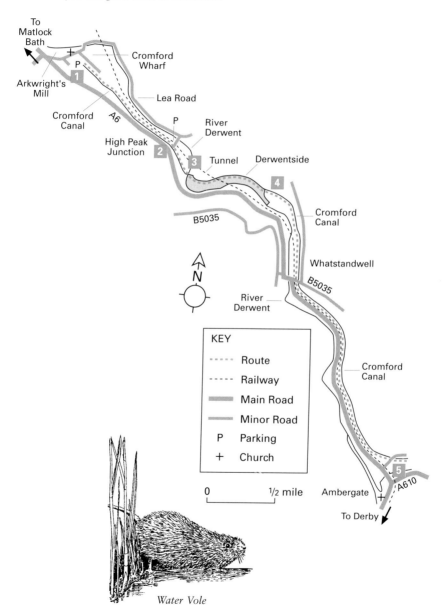

KEY

-----	Route
- - -	Railway
▬▬▬	Main Road
▬▬▬	Minor Road
P	Parking
+	Church

0   ½ mile

Water Vole

Crich Chase and Cromford Canal

A linear walk to do again and again, with something different to see each season. *By Mike and Shirley Cross.*

START/ PARKING:	Ambergate Station car park. Grid ref SK 349517.
DISTANCE:	3½ miles/5.5km.
DIFFICULTY:	An easy linear route, muddy in places.
OS MAP:	1:50,000 sheet 119 Buxton and Matlock.
TOILETS:	None on route.
PUBLIC TRANSPORT:	Trains to Ambergate from Matlock and Derby. Buses stop on the A6 at Ambergate. For more information contact Traveline on 0870 608 2 608.
LOOK FOR:	Woodland birds and water voles all year round. Siskins on the alders in winter. Wood anemone and bluebells in spring. Damselflies on the canal in summer. During autumn, enjoy the wonderful autumn colours along the valley.

Nuthatch

1 Walk down Station Approach to the A610, cross over and turn left under the railway bridge to the A6. Turn right and after 250 metres turn right into Chase Road.

2 On reaching the Cromford Canal bridge cross the stile and turn left along the canal towpath. This section of the canal is a Derbyshire Wildlife Trust nature reserve. *Look for water voles here all year round, and for dragonflies and grass snakes in summer.*

3 Pass under the first canal bridge and in about 1 mile turn right over the next canal bridge into the wood. Follow the signposted track to the left which then goes up the hill towards Whatstandwell, passing Thurlowbooth Farm on your left. In 600 metres you reach the walled garden of Chase Cliffe on the right - at the end of the wall follow the waymarked path up the steep slope to the right. The stile at the top takes you onto the B5035. Turn right and in 300 metres, just before the copse, turn right again onto the footpath over the field.

4 As the wall on your left turns left the footpath heads diagonally left across the field through three squeeze stiles to Chadwick Nick Lane. Turn right. In 60 metres, as the road goes left, take the footpath to the right with the wall on your left. As the path turns left over a stile you have wonderful views over the Derwent Valley to Alport Heights, Black Rocks and Riber.

5 Follow the waymarked path down through Crich Chase, passing through a clearing. *In summer you may glimpse a common lizard sunning itself on the edge of the bracken.* Follow the path which can be very muddy here, downhill, ignoring the track off to the left. Cross the stile into a field and then through the gate and over the bridge to rejoin the canal. Turn right under the bridge to retrace the route to the station via Chase Road and the A6.

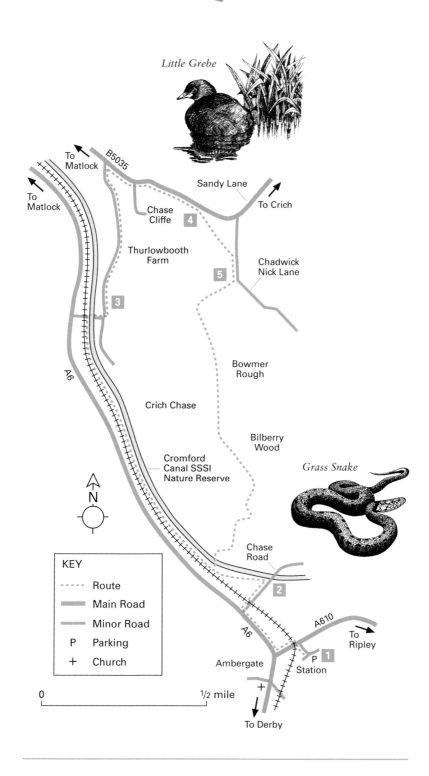

Little Grebe

To Matlock
B5035
To Matlock
Sandy Lane
To Crich
Chase Cliffe **4**
Thurlowbooth Farm
Chadwick Nick Lane
5
3
A6
Bowmer Rough
Crich Chase
Bilberry Wood
Cromford Canal SSSI Nature Reserve

Grass Snake

Chase Road
2

KEY
- - - Route
━━ Main Road
━ Minor Road
P Parking
+ Church

N

A610
To Ripley
A6
Ambergate
Station
P **1**
+

0 — — — — ½ mile

To Derby

Belper and Wyver Lane

Enjoy a pleasant linear walk from the historic mill town of Belper, passing one of the Trust's best birdwatching sites. *By Mike and Shirley Cross.*

START/ PARKING: Belper River Gardens car park - pay and display. Grid ref SK 345482.

DISTANCE: 2 miles/3.2km.

DIFFICULTY: Easy.

OS MAP: 1:50,000 sheet 119 Buxton and Matlock.

Lapwing

TOILETS: At start.

PUBLIC TRANSPORT: Stagecoach East Midlands Service 142 runs between Ambergate and Belper. For details phone Traveline on 0870 608 2 608. There are railway stations at Ambergate and Belper - for details of train times tel: 08457 484950.

LOOK FOR: Little owl at dusk on Whitewells Lane; Daubenton's bats at Halfpenny Bridge on summer nights.

1 From the car park walk up to the A6 and turn right to the traffic lights. The red brick East Mill building is currently home to Derbyshire Wildlife Trust. Turn right, cross the River Derwent and then turn right into Belper Lane.

2 Either turn right into Wyver Lane and follow the single track road for just over 1/2 mile, or take the third right into The Scotches and continue onto the footpath over fields to Wyver Lane. The Trust's reserve can be viewed from the road. *The reserve is important in late summer and winter for its wildfowl and waders such as lapwing, teal and wigeon.*

3 Continue along the track for around 1/2 mile, following the Derwent Valley Heritage Way. Where the track turns right to the farm follow the footpath, forking left through the gate, then go round the wood and left up the hill, crossing two stiles to reach Whitewells Road. Turn right along the lane for 1/2 mile to the T junction with Holly Lane.

4 Cross over and enter The Birches (Woodland Trust) and take any of the paths to the right to rejoin Holly Lane at the bottom of the hill, continuing over the river to the A6. Bus and train services are available for return to Belper or you can retrace your steps.

Speckled Wood Butterfly

Wyver Lane Nature Reserve

The Trust's Wyver Lane Nature Reserve is one of our most important wetland reserves. It has many resident bird species including Canada geese, tufted duck and little grebe. Throughout the year, the numbers of birds are swelled by seasonal visitors, from curlew in spring to various gull species in winter. To protect the many bird species on the reserve there is no access, but there is plenty of opportunity to view the birds from the lane itself, and permits can be purchased for the hide.

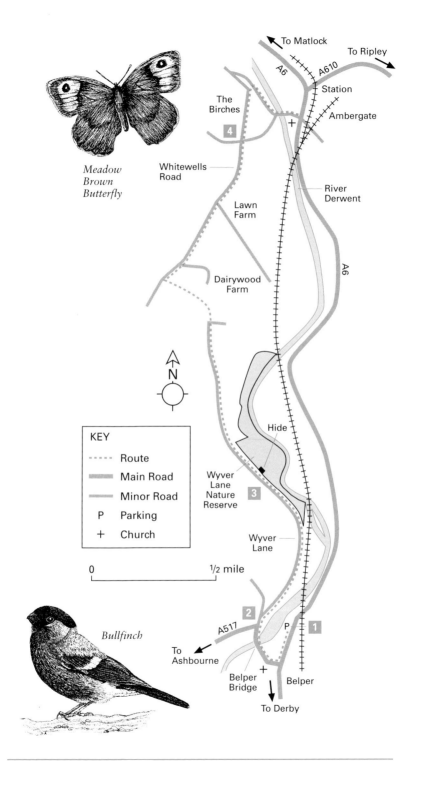

Meadow
Brown
Butterfly

To Matlock
To Ripley
A6
A610
Station
The
Birches
Ambergate
4
Whitewells
Road
River
Derwent
Lawn
Farm
A6
Dairywood
Farm

N

Hide

KEY

- - - - - Route
▬▬▬ Main Road
▬▬▬ Minor Road
P   Parking
+   Church

Wyver
Lane
Nature
Reserve
3

Wyver
Lane

0   ½ mile

Bullfinch

2

A517

P   **1**

To
Ashbourne

Belper
Bridge

Belper

To Derby

Hilton Gravel Pits

An easy-going walk through the South Derbyshire Countryside, with the option of a walk around Hilton Nature Reserve. *By Les Sims.*

START/ PARKING: Willowpit Lane entrance to Hilton Gravel Pits Nature Reserve, adjacent to the junction of the A50 and A516. Grid ref SK 254314.

DISTANCE: 5 miles/8km.

DIFFICULTY: Mostly flat, easy walking on good paths; some road walking. Please keep to the pavements where they exist, otherwise walk on the right facing any traffic.

OS MAP: 1:50,000 sheet 128 Derby and Burton upon Trent.

TOILETS: None on route.

PUBLIC TRANSPORT: Trent Barton services V1 and V2 from Derby to Burton upon Trent call at Hilton.

LOOK FOR: Black poplars; farmland birds.

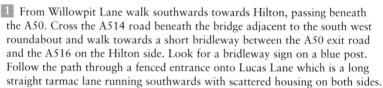

Black Poplar

1 From Willowpit Lane walk southwards towards Hilton, passing beneath the A50. Cross the A514 road beneath the bridge adjacent to the south west roundabout and walk towards a short bridleway between the A50 exit road and the A516 on the Hilton side. Look for a bridleway sign on a blue post. Follow the path through a fenced entrance onto Lucas Lane which is a long straight tarmac lane running southwards with scattered housing on both sides.

2 In half a mile, at the T junction, turn left onto the A5132 Hilton to Willington road, walking past the Don Amott Caravan Centre and the White Swan pub.

3 Opposite Birch Trees Farm and before the old railway bridge, follow the path on the left alongside the bridge where there is a road sign which says Queues Likely. Go through the gates onto the cycle track adjacent to the old railway bridge, turn left to face northwards and walk towards Etwall. Through the arch of the bridge you will see Egginton Station, which is now a private house. *The building with the tall chimney was once Egginton Creamery.* Continue along the cycle path in a northerly direction, passing through a short pedestrian tunnel beneath the A50. Kingfisher Bridge, where kingfishers have been sighted recently, carries the trail across Etwall Brook.
On reaching a new housing development on your right, you are at the site of Etwall Station, which, together with its signal box, was demolished after the railway closed in the 1970s.
The walk passes beneath several brick bridges that have Scots Pines on the approach banks. *These trees were planted to placate the local landowners when the railway was built in 1877. Also earth banks were built to screen the railway from the large houses Ashe Hall and Etwall Hall. The latter was later demolished and now John Port School stands on the site.*

4 After passing under a bridge where there is a seat on the left, pass through a gate and turn right to walk under the Etwall by-pass. Turn left at the red and black National Cycle Network and follow blue and white "68" signs. You are now on the Pennine Cycleway, which runs 355 miles from Derby to Berwick-upon-Tweed via Ashbourne and the Tissington Trail. Follow the track towards the lane at the entrance to Barleyfields Equestrian Centre.

Pass through the barrier turning right in a north-westerly direction towards Sutton-on-the-Hill, again following the "68" signs. On the right you will pass the entrance to the Tara Centre at Ashe Hall where there is an excellent café, open from 10am to 4pm.

Walk along Ash Lane passing Park Farm on your left, and in about 100 metres turn left onto a wide track (marked as a footpath). *Listen out for farmland birds in the hedgerows.* This takes you through to the north end of Willowpit Lane. Turn left at the road and walk back towards Hilton.

5 As you walk along the lane, there is a view of one of the nature reserve's pools on the right, *where you may see water birds such as tufted duck. Look, too, for row of black poplars in the hedge on the left.* If time allows, before returning to your car, go through the gate and into the nature reserve. A network of paths allow for a variety of options to extend your walk.

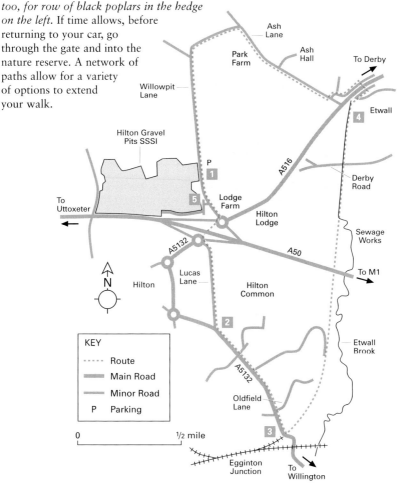

Carvers Rocks

This reserve on the edge of Foremark Reservoir is one of the few remaining parts of lowland Derbyshire where you will find sphagnum moss.
By David and Joanne Hill.

Great Crested Grebe

START/ PARKING:	Foremark Reservoir Visitors' car park. Take the A514 through Ticknall (in the direction of Repton), and after the village turn right, following the signs for Foremark Reservoir. Follow the signs for the car park on the left with the toilets. There is a car parking charge. Grid ref SK 336242.
DISTANCE:	5 miles/8km.
DIFFICULTY:	Moderate. Mainly gravel paths (with some steep steps), meadow areas and a few boggy patches. Some narrow bridges and paths. Care needed when walking along the road near the end.
OS MAP:	1:50,000 sheet 128 Derby and Burton upon Trent.
TOILETS:	At start point in the car park.
PUBLIC TRANSPORT:	Bus services call at Ticknall.
LOOK FOR:	Sphagnum moss on the reserve; farmland birds in winter; wildfowl on the reservoir; dragonflies and butterflies.

1 With the reservoir on your right, leave the car park and walk past the toilet block. You will see footpath signs; follow the Badger walk up the gravelled path. Continue ahead over a grassy section. When you reach a fence turn left, following the footpath to Carvers Rocks and then an immediate right back onto the Badger walk. Continue on this path for some distance, ignoring footpath signs to Scaddows Oaks. This section contains some steep steps. Follow the board walk which is on the edge of the reserve. After the bridge go through the opening in the fence - the Badger walk is now signed to the left. Ignore this and take the right fork onto a grassy track. This leads over a squeeze stile and into the nature reserve.

2 Walk into the reserve, passing the information board, and follow the path until you cross a bridge over a stream. Take the right path (leading straight uphill, not down to the reservoir). Turn right, then down the steps and right at the yellow waymarker. This leads over the bridge and boardwalk, through the wetland area. *This is an area of sphagnum moss, which is very rare in lowland Derbyshire.* Climb up the path and as it begins to drop down, just after the oak tree on the left, take the steps down to the right, this takes you over an area which can remain boggy in the summer and over a small bridge.

3 At the end of the trees you cross a stile out of the reserve and head left up the hill. The next stile takes you across a track which is used for horse training. Go straight across carefully and through the gate (beware of the electric fence) and head towards the edge of the wood on your left. Go through the gate (again crossing the horse training run) and across to the footpath between the fence and the trees. Go through the kissing gate then keep to the left of the field, through the next kissing gate and turn right onto the road. This is a public road but not a through road.

4 Keep following the road, past the radio transmitter and good views to the right. At the very end of the road there is a wooden gate to the left and farm entrance to the right. Go through the gate and follow the track down the hill. *This is a good area to see farmland birds in winter.* After the next gate, follow the road past the farm and houses until you reach the Ticknall to Milton road.

5 Turn right onto the road (CAUTION: this is a busy, fast road - please take care). Follow the road past the Fishing and Sailing entrance and take the entrance on the right back into the Visitors Car parks.

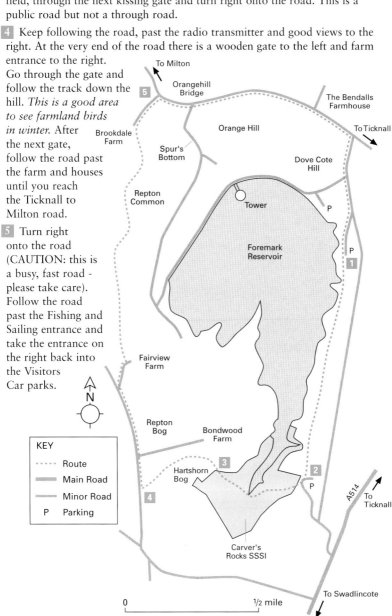

To Milton

Orangehill Bridge

5

The Bendalls Farmhouse

Orange Hill

To Ticknall

Brookdale Farm

Spur's Bottom

Dove Cote Hill

Repton Common

Tower

P

Foremark Reservoir

P

1

Fairview Farm

N

Repton Bog

Bondwood Farm

Hartshorn Bog

3

P

2

A514

To Ticknall

4

Carver's Rocks SSSI

KEY
- ⋯⋯ Route
- ▓▓ Main Road
- ▬ Minor Road
- P Parking

0   ½ mile

To Swadlincote

Contact Us

Derbyshire Wildlife Trust
East Mill, Belper
Derbyshire DE56 1XH
Tel: 01773 881188
Fax: 01773 821826
Email: enquiries@derbyshirewt.co.uk
www.derbyshirewildlifetrust.org.uk

Whistlestop Centre
Old Railway Station
Matlock Bath
Derbyshire DE4 3PT
Tel: 01629 580958
Email: whistlestop@derbyshirewt.co.uk

NEIGHBOURING WILDLIFE TRUSTS

The Wildlife Trust for Lancashire, Manchester and North Merseyside
The Barn, Berkeley Drive, Preston
Lancs PR5 6BY
Tel: 01772 324129
Email: lancswt@cix.co.uk

Leicestershire and Rutland Wildlife Trust
Brocks Hill Environment Centre
Washbrook Lane, Oadby
Leicestershire LE2 5JJ
Tel: 0116 270444
Email: info@lrwt.org.uk

Nottinghamshire Wildlife Trust
The Old Ragged School
Brook Street
Nottingham NG1 1EA
Tel: 0115 958 8242
Email: nottswt@cix.co.uk

Sheffield Wildlife Trust
37 Stafford Road
Sheffield S2 2SF
Tel: 0114 263 4335
Email: mail@wildsheffield.com

Staffordshire Wildlife Trust
Wolseley Centre, Wolseley Bridge
Nr Rugeley, Stafford ST17 0WT
Tel: 01889 880100
Email: staffswt@cix.co.uk

Yorkshire Wildlife Trust
1 St George's Place, Todcaster Rd
York YO24 1GN
Tel: 01904 659570
Email: yorkshirewt@cix.co.uk

The Wildlife Trusts UK Office
The Kiln, Waterside
Mather Road, Newark
Nottinghamshire NG24 1WT
Tel: 0870 0367711
Email: enquiry@wildlifetrusts.org
www.wildlifetrusts.org

OTHER ORGANISATIONS

Derbyshire County Council
County Hall, Matlock
Derbyshire DE4 3AG
Tel: 01629 580000

Natural England
Endcliffe, Deepdale Business Park
Ashford Road, Bakewell
Derbyshire DE45 1GT
Tel: 01629 815095

National Trust
East Midlands Region
Clumber Park Stableyard
Worksop
Nottinghamshire S80 3BE
Tel: 01909 486411

Peak District National Park Authority
Aldern House
Baslow Road
Bakewell
Derbyshire DE45 1AE

Severn Trent Water
2297 Coventry Road
Birmingham B26 3PU

Derbyshire Wildlife Trust Publications

*A*lso available from Derbyshire Wildlife Trust:

Wildlife Gardening by Fran Hill
Inspiration and advice for
the wildlife gardener.
£7.95

Nature Reserves Guide
Discover the wild side of
Derbyshire with detailed maps
and easy to follow descriptions
of our nature reserves.
£9.95

The above publications can be ordered direct from:

Derbyshire Wildlife Trust, East Mill, Bridge Foot, Belper, Derbyshire DE56 1XH.

Please make cheques payable to:
Derbyshire Wildlife Resources - prices shown include postage and packing.

We also produce a variety of factsheets on wildlife gardening,
advice to landowners and species information.
For more details contact us on 01773 881188 for a publications list
or visit our website, www.derbyshirewildlifetrust.org.uk

Join Us

*D*erbyshire Wildlife Trust is the county's leading wildlife organisation. We protect wildlife throughout Derbyshire by...

- Managing nature reserves supporting Derbyshire's unique diversity of habitats and species.

- Conserving threatened species, ensuring that the rich variety of wildlife in the county remains for future generations.

- Working with people, to raise awareness of our role in protecting the environment.

- Involving people - the future of Derbyshire's wildlife is in our hands, you can make a difference by joining us.

Benefits of membership

- Regular newsletters, full of up-to-date news and features and Natural World magazine.

- Opportunities to get involved in a wide range of events - guided walks, work parties, talks etc.

- The chance to meet new people through local groups and Trust activities.

To find out more about joining us
contact us on
01773 881188
or click on to
www.derbyshirewildlifetrust.org.uk

Take a walk on the wild side.

16 routes from $1^{1}/_{2}$ miles to 13 miles.
Detailed route descriptions around
Derbyshire Wildlife Trust nature reserves.
Tips on when to go and wildlife to look for.

Published by Derbyshire Wildlife Trust.

The publication of this guide has been supported by

AGGREGATE
INDUSTRIES

£6.50